Flip-up
Bulletin Boards

by Muriel Feldshuh

RATNER MEDIA AND TECHNOLOGY CENTER
JEWISH EDUCATION CENTER OF CLEVELAND

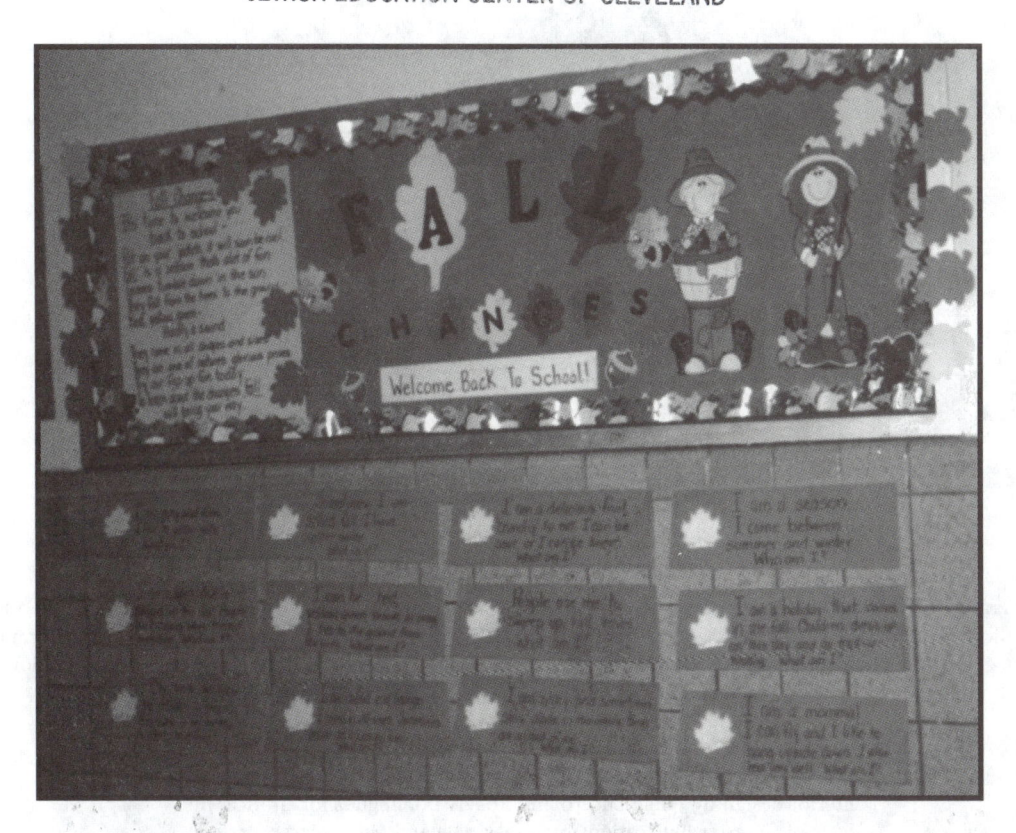

SCHOLASTIC
PROFESSIONAL BOOKS

New York ■ Toronto ■ London ■ Auckland ■ Sydney

Dedication

This book is dedicated to the memory of my father, Louis, who would have been very proud, and to my mother for her support throughout the years.

Acknowledgments

Thanks to Mickey Revenaugh and Terry Cooper for taking an interest in my work and pointing me in the right direction. A special thank-you to my editor, Deborah Schecter, for her patience and help, and for being there for me whenever I called. And to Steven, thanks for your love and patience.

Scholastic grants teachers permission to photocopy the reproducible pages from this book for classroom use. No other part of this publication may be reproduced in whole or part, or stored in a retrieval system, or transmitted in any form or by any means, electronic, photocopying, recording, or otherwise, without permission of the publisher. For information regarding permission, write to Scholastic Professional Books, 555 Broadway, New York, NY 10012-3999.

Cover design by Vincent Ceci and Jaime Lucero
Cover photo by Donelly Marks
Interior design by Jaime Lucero and Robert Dominguez for Grafica, Inc.
Interior illustrations by James Hale and Mona Marks
Poems by Helen H. Moore and Muriel Feldshuh
Photos by Muriel Feldshuh

ISBN 0-590-74393-7
Copyright © 1996 by Muriel Feldshuh
All rights reserved
Printed in the U.S.A.

12 11 10 9 8 7 6 5 4 3 2   6 7 8 9/9/01/0

Table of Contents

Introduction 4

September
- Fall Changes 9
- Apples: What a Treat! Good to Eat! 12

October
- Fire Safety Is a Must 15
- Batmania 18

November
- Giving Thanks 21
- Books Change Lives 24

December
- Going Places 26
- Holidays Around the World 28

January
- Celebrate With Hats 30
- We Have Dreams, Too! 32

February
- President's Month 34
- Let's Be Heart Smart 36

March
- Women in History 38
- Buzzing With Insects! 40

April
- Get Well Soon, Planet Earth! 43
- Animals in Danger 45

May
- Keep Fit and Healthy 47
- Know Your Safety Signs 50

June
- Celebrating Our Flag 52
- I Want to Leave You Laughing 54

Introduction

◢ What Are Flip-ups?

Using only construction paper and the simplest of supplies, you can provide meaningful opportunities for children to interact with bulletin board displays that support your curriculum. The key to these special bulletin boards are flip-ups: questions, riddles, or definitions written on the outside of a folded piece of construction paper. A child simply flips up the paper to find the answer or vocabulary word inside. The flip-up format is a great way to promote reading and learning about topics like endangered animals, fire safety, health and fitness—the possibilities are limitless! The format also presents an enjoyable challenge for children across grade levels.

Where did the idea for flip-ups come from? Working both as a classroom and library teacher in a Brooklyn, New York, public elementary school, I was determined to make the curriculum hard to resist. Over the years, I have been fascinated by the way students have been drawn to various bulletin boards I created. I tried to make displays that would produce an immediate visual connection. I wanted my students to interact with the information before them. I soon realized that while my bulletin boards were highly regarded by many students, there were still some children who did not connect with them.

Several years ago, after creating hundreds of bulletin boards, I met with some success when I placed "flip-up" facts below or directly on the bulletin board, which could be used independently or read aloud and shared by students. The flip-ups encouraged children to get involved and risk an answer to a riddle or an interesting question. The device produced exciting results. A right answer to a riddle, for example, would bring a rewarding smile to the face of a child passing my hallway bulletin board and motivate that child to look more carefully and critically at it. Other teachers soon brought their classes to visit the bulletin board and practice using flip-ups. Parents and visitors to the school also expressed their interest in my flip-up creations and became devoted fans, coming by each month to see my latest collection.

To share my work with others, I took photographs of my bulletin board displays and organized my ideas into this book. I have included two suggested topics for each school month from September through June, along with basic instructions for making the bulletin boards and flip-ups. In each section you'll find photographs of the bulletin boards, ideas for expanding the bulletin board topics with your students, and ways to use the flip-ups with different grade levels. As I worked on this book, I adapted and added to my original flip-ups and poems. I hope that you too will feel free to adapt or expand upon what I've done and that my ideas capture your imagination. Have fun and experiment!

Choosing a Bulletin Board Site

Flip-ups can go anywhere: in a hallway, library, or classroom learning center. Because the flip-ups themselves are taped to the wall around the bulletin board, you'll want to choose a spot with enough wall space.

Making the Flip-up Bulletin Boards

Each flip-up bulletin board will look different, but they will all share the same basic elements. Follow these basic steps to make each board; you'll find specific ideas for colors, shapes, and flip-ups in each section.

1. THE BACKGROUND
Staple fadeless construction paper to the bulletin board to create a background for each topic. Select a color that matches the topic—for example, red or green for the "Apples" board.

2. THE BORDER
Each bulletin board features a colorful border that ties in with the theme. You and your students can make the borders from construction paper, or you can purchase premade bordettes at a teacher supply store.

3. THE TITLE
Write the title of each theme board in large letters and staple it to the top of the bulletin board area. Use the titles I've suggested, or have fun coming up with your own.

4. THE POEM
The centerpiece of each bulletin board is a poem that introduces each theme. Write the poem on a large piece of oaktag, and staple it to the center of the bulletin board. I've included poetry suggestions for each topic; you may wish to write your own, or have your students write them.

5. STUDENTS' ARTWORK
One way to get students involved with the bulletin boards is to have them create theme-related artwork or projects that you staple to the bulletin board area. I've included specific suggestions throughout the book.

6. THE FLIP-UPS
To make a basic flip-up, fold a piece of construction paper in half lengthwise. On the outside flap, write the question, riddle, or definition (I've given specific suggestions for each topic). Write the answer or term on the inside. Use masking tape to attach the flip-ups to the wall underneath the bulletin board.

The hard center of an apple / Core

7. INSTRUCTION CARDS

Are these statements true or false?

Flip up the card to find out!

Make one extra flip-up or card that tells students how to use the flip-ups. (For example: "Are these statements true or false? Flip up the card to find out!"). Attach the instruction cards to the wall or bulletin board near the flip-up area.

Making the Flip-ups Fun

■ Decorate the outside flap of the flip-ups with a theme-related sticker (for example, an Earth Day sticker for a display about the environment).

■ Try making flip-ups in fun shapes. You'll find suggestions and templates (for example, a firefighter's helmet for fire safety, a butterfly for insects) throughout the book. Feel free to adapt my ideas and come up with your own!

Ways to Use the Flip-ups

■ To help students practice independent reading, have children read the flip-ups by themselves.

■ Have students work with partners: One student reads the riddle or question, and the other gives the answer.

■ Students can create an alphabetized glossary of different terms presented on the flip-ups.

■ Encourage students to make their own flip-up questions. Feature different sets of questions during each week of the month.

■ Students can make up their own riddles for the flip-ups. Many of the topics mentioned in this book lend themselves to riddles (for example, bats, fall, and hats).

■ Scramble words on the outside of flip-ups, and have students try to unscramble them. The solution goes on the inside flap.

■ In addition to the holiday suggestions in the book, have students create flip-ups for other holidays, such as Valentine's Day or Groundhog Day.

■ Make a class flip-up set. Have each student write his or her name on the outside flap and a theme-related tip or suggestion on the inside (for example, an idea for saving the environment, or a favorite book or author).

■ After students have studied the flip-ups for a topic, reverse the flip-ups so that the term or answer is on the outside. See if students can tell what the definition or question is on the inside.

■ Save all the flip-ups, and use them as a game or review at the end of the school year.

📄 Using the Flip-ups at Different Grade Levels

In each section you'll find specific suggestions for extending the flip-up topics for younger and older students.

📄 A Note on the Photographs

The photographs that accompany each section will give you an idea of how each bulletin board might look. In many cases I have made changes to my original ideas, so the flip-ups or poems in the photos may be different than those that appear in the book—just another indication of how flexible and adaptable these bulletin boards can be!

September • October • November • December • January • February • March • April • May • June

Fall Changes

This back-to-school bulletin board is a great way to introduce students to the flip-up concept. The changing seasons, fall sports, and school are topics that can be used to complete the theme.

Getting Started

The seasons bring different kinds of changes to different regions of North America. After reading the poem "Fall Changes," below, discuss the changes in nature—and in their own lives—that students notice in the fall.

Bulletin Board Poem

FALL CHANGES

Fall is here.
Another year
is coming to an end.
Summer's finished.
Summer's gone.
Winter's 'round the bend.
Fall is piles of crunchy leaves,
orange, gold, and red.
Fall is sweaters, with long sleeves,
and blankets on the bed.
Fall is football.
Fall is pumpkins.
Fall's where summer ends,
and fall is coming back to school
and seeing all my friends.

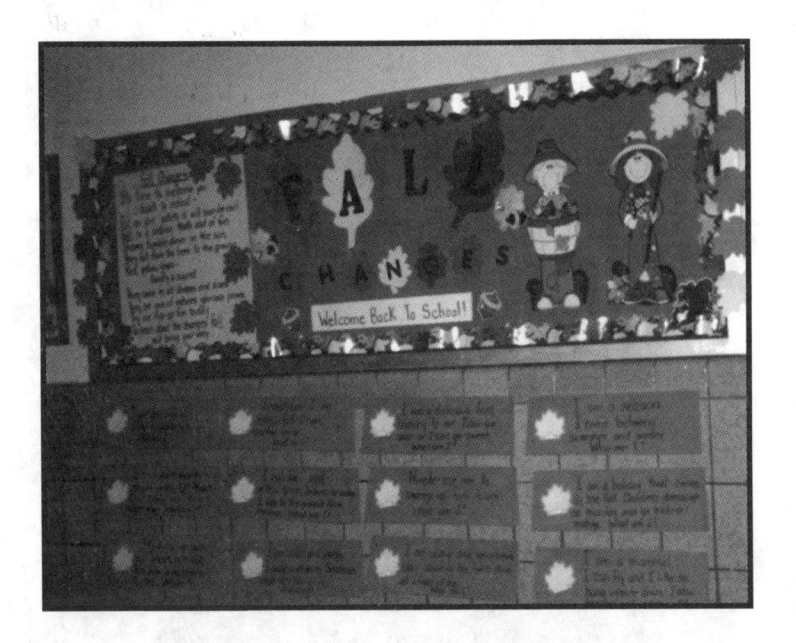

Bulletin Board Tips

■ Write each letter of the title on a piece of paper shaped like a leaf.

■ Use fall colors such as orange, brown, and yellow for the background, flip-ups, and border.

■ Use the leaf template on page 11 for a fun flip-up shape. Then have students write their names on real leaves and decorate the board with them.

Flip-up Ideas

Students will love solving these fun fall riddles.

[Instruction Card] *Can you solve these fall riddles? Lift the flaps to find the answers!*

- I stay at my post each day and night. When birds see me, they get a fright. What am I?
A scarecrow

- I'm yellow and black on the outside, and I'm filled with students on the inside. What am I?
A school bus

- What is a snake's favorite subject in school? **Hiss-tory**

- I'm busy gathering nuts all day. When I'm done, I'll store them away. What am I? **A squirrel**

- I'm made of rubber, but I'm more powerful than lead! What am I?
An eraser

- I'm a sport people like to play. When there's a touchdown, they scream "Hooray!" What am I?
Football

- My pages are blank when the school year is new, but they're all filled up when the year is through. What am I? **A notebook**

- In summer I like to hang around, but when fall comes, I fly to the ground. What am I?
A leaf

- Hungry squirrels love me so, but from me mighty oak trees grow. What am I? **An acorn**

Extensions

Younger Students: Encourage students to write their own fall riddles on flip-ups. Then make a class Big Book with a flip-up riddle on each page.

Older Students: Go on a leaf-collecting expedition in your neighborhood. Challenge students to identify the leaves, using a field guide. Then label them and add them to the bulletin board.

Suggested Book Links

Exploring Autumn by Sandra Markle (Atheneum, 1991). Besides giving an excellent explanation of fall and the changes this season brings, you'll find riddles, games, and other wonderful fall activities to do with students.

Why Do Leaves Change Color? by Betsy Maestro (HarperCollins, 1994). Readers find out how leaves change color and what happens to a tree as it gets ready for winter. The fall colors in this book are breathtaking.

LEAF TEMPLATE

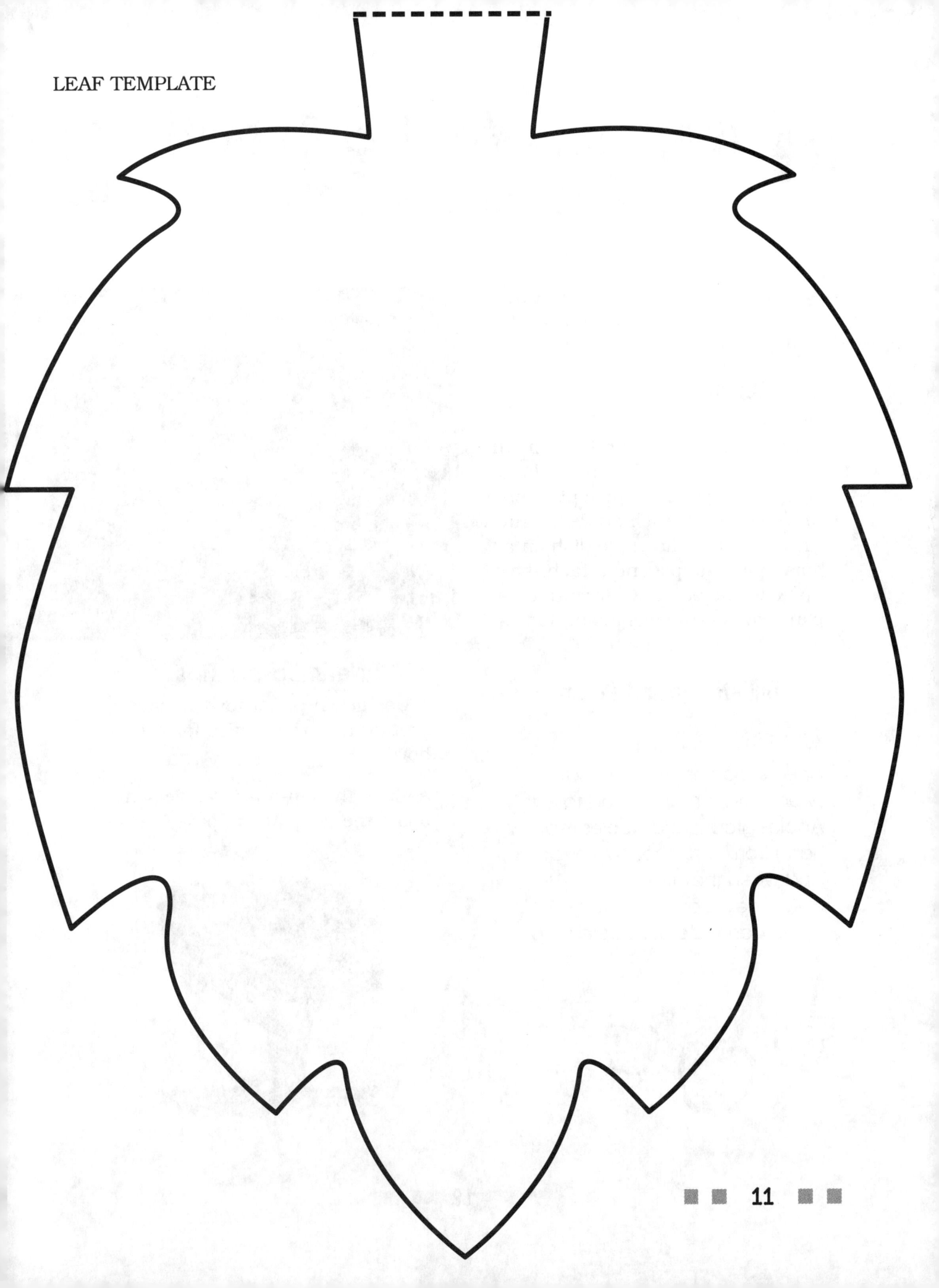

Apples: What a Treat! Good to Eat!

This bulletin board is a fun way to practice apple-related vocabulary words.

Getting Started

Read the poem "Apples." Then ask younger students to brainstorm all the different ways apples can be eaten—applesauce, apple pie, apple juice, etc. Have each student write his or her favorite apple dish on a small paper apple and attach the apple to the board. Older students can brainstorm facts about apples and add those to the board.

Bulletin Board Poem

APPLES

Apples, apples, what a treat,
sweet and tart and good to eat.
Apples green, and apples red,
hang from branches overhead.
And when they ripen,
down they drop,
so we can taste our apple crop!

Bulletin Board Tips

- Use green paper for the background and red apples for the border.

- Make the flip-ups in apple shapes using the template on page 14.

Flip-up Ideas

You can adjust the difficulty of the vocabulary here to match your students' abilities.

[Instruction Card] *Use the clues to figure out these apple words. The answers are under the flaps.*

- A place where many apple trees are planted **Orchard**

- The hard center of an apple **Core**

- A special drink made from apples **Cider**

- What an apple is before it becomes fruit **A blossom**

- The part of the apple that holds it to the branch **The stem**

- To pick apples at the end of the growing season **Harvest**

- The season when apples are ready to pick **Autumn**

- He planted apple seeds across the United States **Johnny Appleseed**

Extensions

Younger Students: Use apples as a basis for teaching following directions. Make a simple apple recipe in class, and have students write down the steps in order afterward.

Older Students: Challenge students to do some detective work to find out how the apples in your school cafeteria get there. Where are they grown? How far do they travel? Are apples grown in your state?

Suggested Book Links

The Life and Times of the Apple by Charles Micucci (Orchard, 1992). Apple facts, apple science, apple math, and even apple lore can be found in this comprehensive, beautifully illustrated book.

Picking Apples and Pumpkins by Amy and Richard Hutchings (Scholastic, 1994). Beautiful photos bring the pastime of apple picking to life for young readers.

APPLE
TEMPLATE

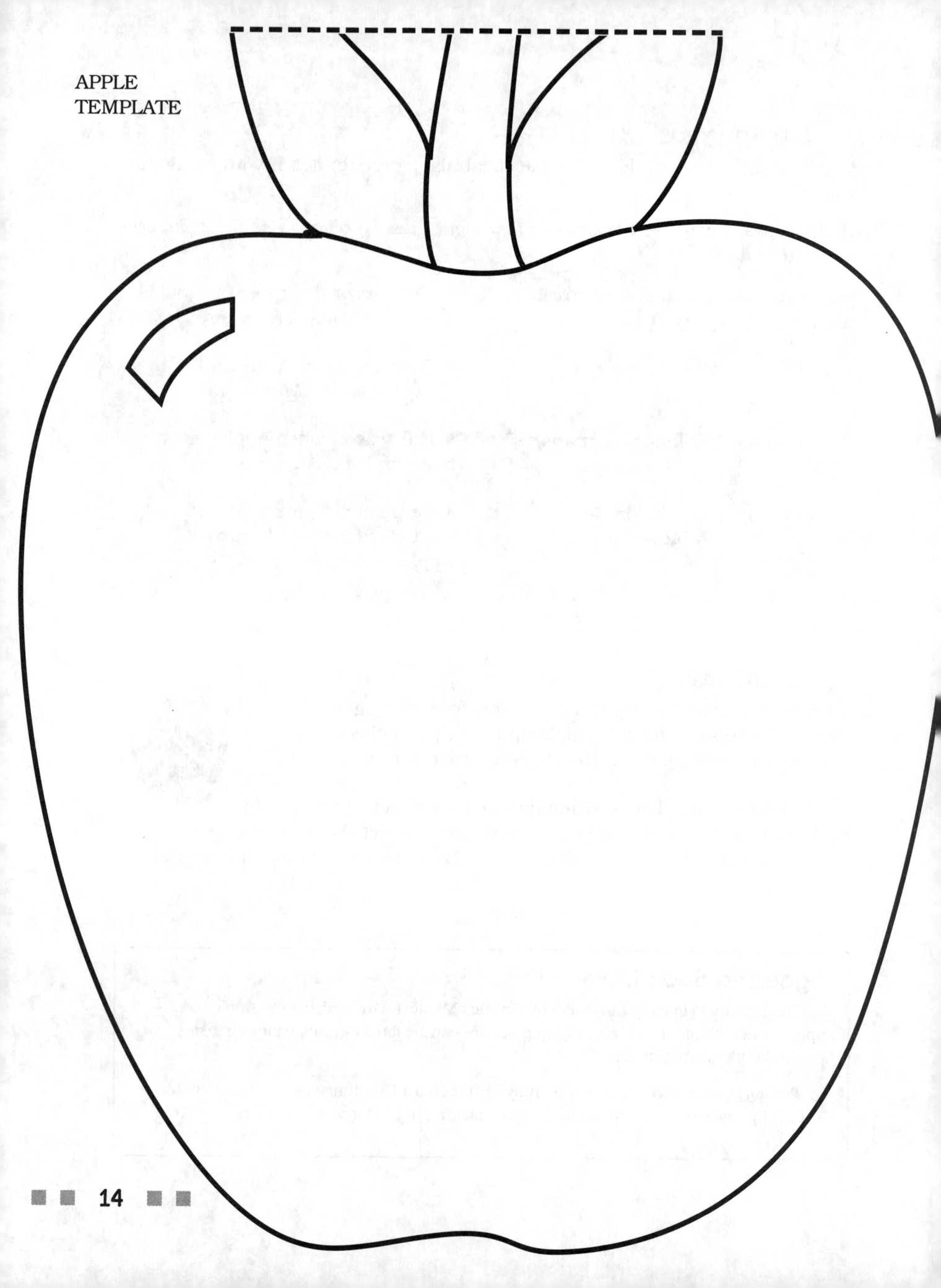

14

Fire Safety Is a Must

October is National Fire Safety Month. This bulletin board helps students learn and reinforce important fire safety skills.

Getting Started

Read the poem and go over basic fire safety rules with your students. Use the fire helmet template on page 17 to make flip-ups for each student. Have each student write his or her name on the outside and a fire safety rule on the inside. Staple these helmets to the bulletin board.

Bulletin Board Poem

FIRE SAFETY

Fire can be useful
to cook our food with heat,
to keep our houses warm and give us
something hot to eat.
But fire can be harmful—
it can be a deadly foe.
So fire safety rules are something
everyone should know.

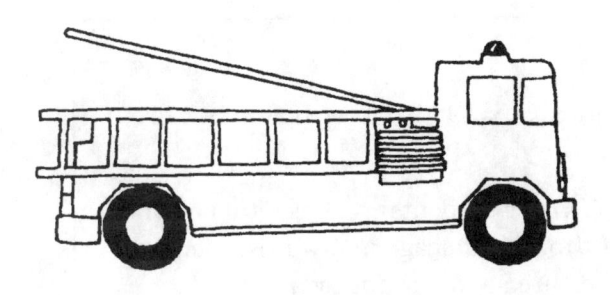

Bulletin Board Tips

- Use white construction paper for the background and red for the border. The students' individual flip-ups can be made with yellow construction paper.

- Use the fire helmet template on page 17 to make the flip-ups.

- If you have photos or pictures of firefighters, add them to the bulletin board.

Flip-up Ideas

These flip-ups will help children review fire safety rules.

[Instruction Card] *Can you answer these questions about fire safety? Lift the flaps to find the answers!*

- If there is smoke in a room, what should you do? **Drop to the ground and crawl under the smoke.**

- If you hear a fire alarm ring, what should you do? **Walk to the nearest exit and wait for instructions from an adult.**

- How many smoke detectors should you have in your house? **Two: One outside bedrooms and one near the kitchen.**

- Why do electrical appliances need to be checked often? **To make sure the plugs are in good condition.**

- When should you STOP! DROP! and ROLL? **If your clothing catches on fire.**

- Why should you practice fire drills in your house? **To know how to exit if there is a fire.**

- What should you do if you find matches or a lighter? **You should give them to an adult.**

- How do you report a fire? **Call 911.**

- Why do smoke detectors need to be checked often? **To make sure the batteries are still working.**

Extensions

Younger Students: Contact a local firehouse to see if a firefighter might be willing to come to your classroom to speak about fire safety. Or see if you can arrange a class trip to the nearest firehouse in your neighborhood.

Older Students: Have students make a map showing the best way to exit their home in case of a fire.

Suggested Book Links

Fire Trucks by Hope Irvin Marston (Dodd, Mead & Co., 1984). This book about fire engines may spark a new bulletin board on their history!

The Great Fire by Jim Murphy (Scholastic, 1995). Older students will enjoy this Newbery Honor book that tells the story of the fire that swept through Chicago in 1871. Readers will get a better understanding of why fire safety standards are so important today.

FIRE HELMET TEMPLATE

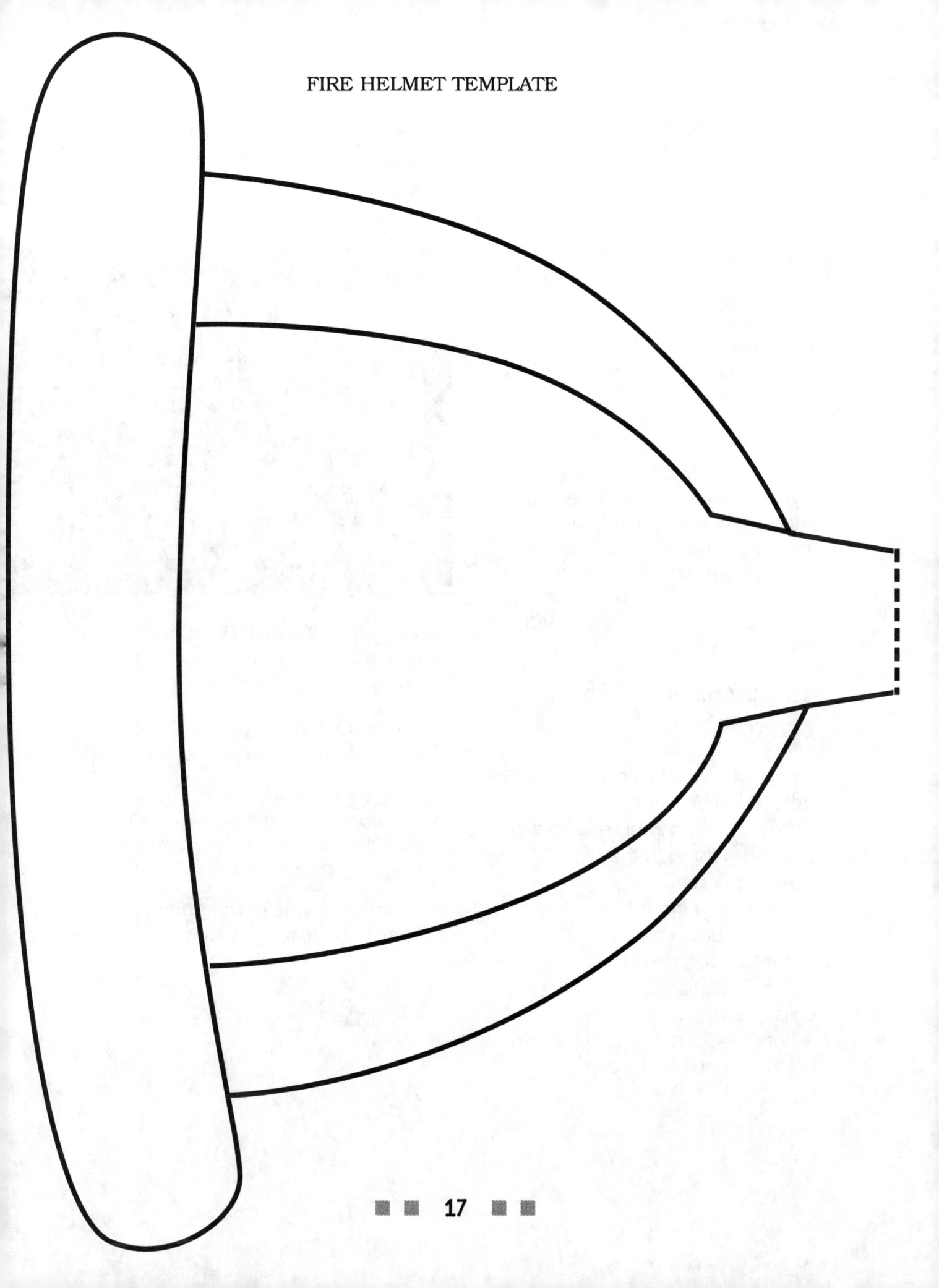

17

Batmania

In October, students' minds are preoccupied with all kinds of creepy creatures. This bulletin board is a great opportunity to learn the real facts about bats, those mysterious creatures of the night.

Getting Started

Most students will need some background on bats before interacting with the flip-ups. Read the poem. Then list what students already know about bats. Afterward, read aloud a book about bats (see suggestions on page 19). How many of their conceptions were true?

Bulletin Board Poem

BATS
All around the classroom,
bats are everywhere.
Bats on books and bulletin boards
and flying through the air!
Hanging around,
together in a crowd
With their upsides down,
(oh those bats are loud!)
Bats in the belfry,
bats in every nook.
Want to learn more about them?
Lift these flaps and look!

Bulletin Board Tips

- Use white paper for the background and black for the border.

- Use the bat template on page 20 to make the flip-ups.

- If you use black paper for the flip-ups, put white paper inside so that you can write the answer or use gray paper instead.

- Write the title of the bulletin board in a giant bat shape.

Flip-up Ideas

Your students will go batty over these true-or-false questions.

[Instruction Card] *Are these statements about bats true or false? Lift the flaps to find out!*

- Bats are birds. **False. They're mammals.**

- Bats are blind. **False. They can see, but they use their powerful hearing to help them find their way.**

- Bats live all over the world. **True**

- All bats are the same size. **False. Some are as small as insects; others are bigger than you when they spread their wings!**

- The bodies of most bats are covered with fur. **True**

- Bats are pests. **False. In fact, bats eat pesty bugs.**

- Bats like to hang upside down. **True**

- All bats live in caves. **False. Some live in caves, and others live in attics, trees, and even under plants.**

- Bats are most active during the night. **True. They're called nocturnal animals.**

- Bats often attack humans. **False. They are very gentle and rarely bite unless frightened or sick.**

Extensions

Younger Students: Bats are a good lead-in for a discussion about classifying animals. How are mammals different from birds? Why is a bat considered a mammal? Show students pictures of different kinds of animals, and challenge them to classify them.

Older Students: Invite students to research different types of bats and create a "bat mobile" by drawing and labeling their favorites, then hanging them with string from a coat hanger.

Suggested Book Links

Bats: Night Fliers by Betsy Maestro (Scholastic, 1994). Filled with maps, diagrams, and detailed illustrations, this book is an excellent overview of bats.

Stellaluna by Janell Cannon (Harcourt Brace, 1993). This popular picture book tells the charming story of a lost young bat who is raised by birds.

BAT TEMPLATE

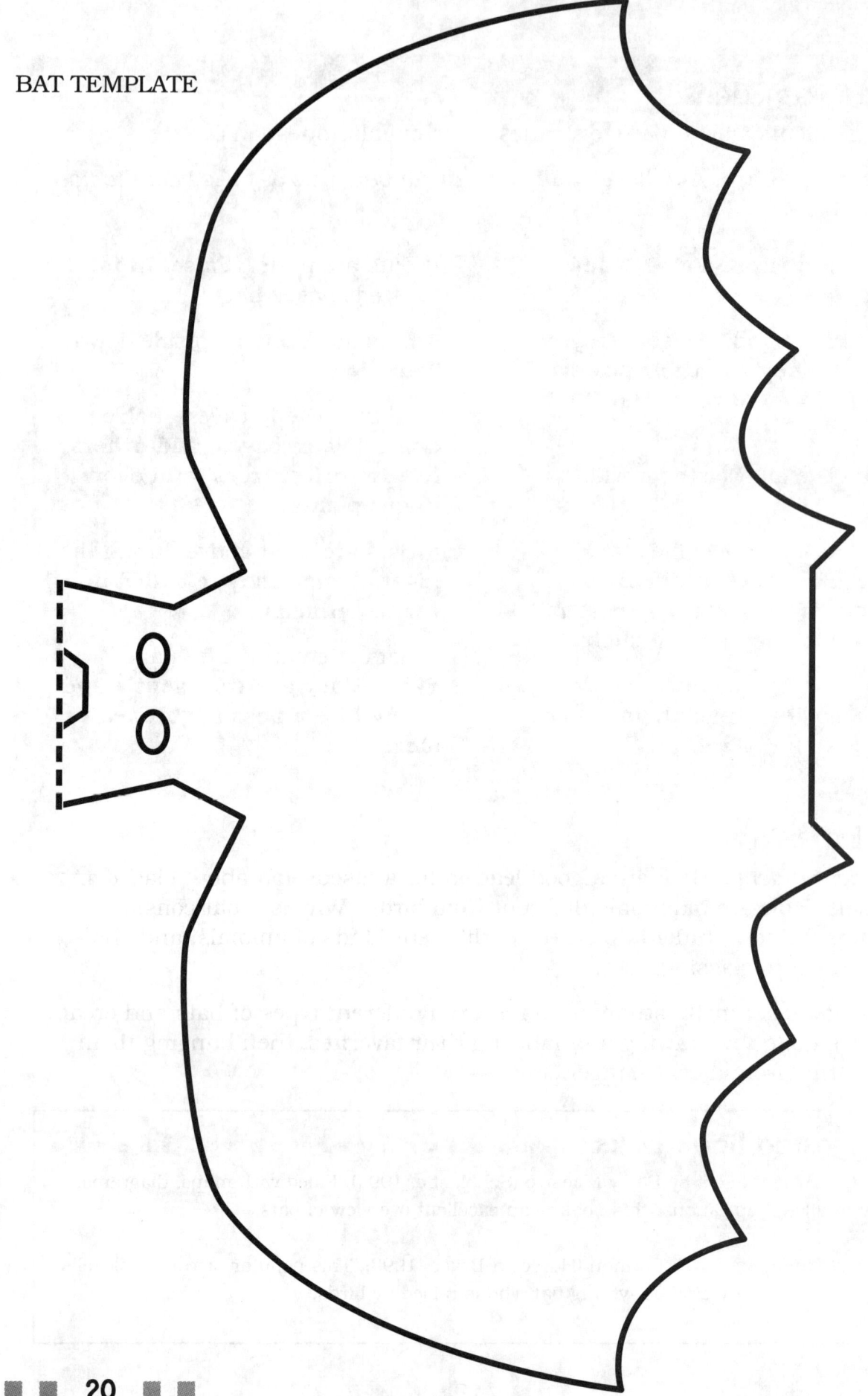

ptember • October • **November** • December • January • February • March • April • May • June

Giving Thanks

This bulletin board provides a natural centerpiece for your yearly Thanksgiving activities.

Getting Started

Write the poem on the chalkboard or on a piece of oaktag, leaving the underlined words blank. Ask students to fill in the poem with familiar Thanksgiving words.

Bulletin Board Poem

GIVING THANKS

Gobble up your <u>turkey</u>.
Eat the stuffing and cranberries, too.
It's time for sharing with your friends
And being glad that you are you.
Be <u>thankful</u> for your family
Your school and home and such.
Remember the <u>Pilgrims</u> and Indians.
They were brave and did so much.
It's <u>harvest</u> time and fall is here
Be thankful for all you hold so dear.

Bulletin Board Tips

- Use orange paper for the background and brown for the border.

- Make the flip-ups in turkey shapes using the template on page 23. Glue feathers to the tail for a realistic effect.

- Make smaller flip-ups in pumpkin shapes. Have students write their names on the outside and something they are thankful for on the inside. Use these to decorate the board.

21

📄 Flip-up Ideas

Students will enjoy filling in the blanks to complete these Thanksgiving facts.

[Instruction Card] *Which words will fill in the blanks in these sentences? Lift the flaps to find out!*

- The Pilgrims came to America from _____.
England

- The Pilgrims traveled to America on a ship called the _____.
Mayflower

- Native Americans helped the Pilgrims plant _____.
corn

- The Native Americans invited to the first Thanksgiving were members of the _____ tribe.
Wampanoag

- The first Thanksgiving was held in the state of _____.
Massachusetts

- The first Thanksgiving was held in the year _____.
1621

- President _____ proclaimed Thanksgiving a national holiday in 1863.
Abraham Lincoln

- _____ was eaten at the first Thanksgiving, just like it is today.
Turkey

- Many people give _____ on this holiday.
thanks

- _____ wanted the turkey to be the national bird of the United States, instead of the eagle.
Ben Franklin

📄 Extensions

Younger Students: Re-create the original Thanksgiving celebration with your students. Make costumes and prepare food that might have been found at the first feast.

Older Students: Thanksgiving is a great time to research the history of Native Americans in your state.

Suggested Book Links

Pilgrims: Thematic Unit Developed in Cooperation With the Pilgrim Hall Museum by Susan Moger (Scholastic, 1995). A complete theme unit packed with a rich assortment of hands-on, reproducible activities and background information about the Pilgrims.

Sarah Morton's Day, *Samuel Eaton's Day*, and *Tapenum's Day* by Kate Waters (Scholastic, 1989, 1993, 1996). This classic trilogy takes readers back to the time of the first Thanksgiving, as seen through the eyes of three children. Realistic photographs enhance the text.

TURKEY
TEMPLATE

23

September • October • **November** • December • January • February • March • April • May • Jun

Books Change Lives

Book Week is celebrated in November. I created this bulletin board to spark a discussion on the books that changed my students' lives in some way.

📖 Getting Started

After reading the poem, start a class discussion about books and how they can inspire us and make us think. Ask students to name books that have changed their lives in some way and explain why.

📖 Bulletin Board Poem

BOOKS
If you read a few,
then you'll know it's true:
Books are good for you!
Books of fiction, books of fact,
Books of manners, poise, and tact!
Chefs read cook-books,
Pirates read hook-books,
Little kids read lift-and-look books!
Books of poems and books of prose
Once you've read some of those,
I'm sure you will agree,
Books are good for you and me!

📖 Bulletin Board Tips

■ Use yellow construction paper for the background.

■ Make or buy a border of blue stars to represent the idea that these books are "stars" in children's lives.

■ Make the flip-ups in the shape of an open book.

■ Write the letters of each word in the heading on a piece of paper shaped like a book.

📖 Flip-up Ideas

These flip-ups can be very specific to your students. One idea is to have children write their names on the outside of the flip-ups and the books that inspire them on the inside. You may also wish to base the bulletin board on favorite books in your classroom. Write the book title on the outside and the author's name on the inside. A more general approach, shown here, involves reviewing different genres with children.

[Instruction Card] *Can you name the kind of books these are? Are they fact or fiction? Fairy tales or fables? Lift the flaps to find out!*

- *The Emperor's New Clothes* by Hans Christian Anderson **Fairy tale**

- *Sarah Morton's Day* by Kate Waters **Historical fiction**

- *Jesse Owens: Olympic Star* by Patricia McKissack and Frederick McKissack **Biography**

- *The Boy Who Cried Wolf* **Fable**

- *Lost in the Storm* by Carol Carrick **Realistic fiction**

- *Freckle Juice* by Judy Blume **Humorous fiction**

- *A Chair for My Mother* by Vera B. Williams **Picture book**

- *Sharks* by Ann McGovern **Nonfiction**

- *Paul Bunyan* by Steven Kellogg **Tall tale**

- *A Dark Dark Tale* by Ruth Brown **Mystery**

📖 Extensions

Younger Students: Invite students to write letters to the author of one of their favorite books, explaining how the book inspired them. Send the letters in care of the publisher's address, located in the front of the book.

Older Students: Have students imagine that they are presenting their favorite author with an award and write a short tribute to that person. You may wish to have students read their tributes aloud at a class author celebration.

Suggested Book Links

📕 *The Author Studies Handbook* by Laura Kotch and Leslie Zackman (Scholastic, 1996). Topics include organizing an author read-aloud group, and teaching skills and strategies.

📕 *Meet the Authors and Illustrators: 60 Creators of Favorite Children's Books Talk About Their Work, Vols. I and II* by Deborah Kovacs and James Preller (Scholastic, 1991, 1993). Meet Beverly Cleary, Eric Carle, Virginia Hamilton, Anno, Chris Van Allsburg, Jack Prelutsky, and many more popular authors and illustrators!

Going Places

This bulletin board is a great beginning for a classroom geography center.

Getting Started

Use the poem to start a discussion with students about traveling around the world. Which countries have they visited? Which countries would they like to visit if they had the chance? Use pushpins to plot your class's dream destinations on a world map. This is also a great opportunity to practice basic map skills. Which destination is farthest away from your state? Which is closest to water? Which is farthest north?

Bulletin Board Poem

GOING PLACES

Oh, the places we can go!
China . . .
Sweden . . .
Mexico . . .
Get there fast or get there slow!
London . . .
Sydney . . .
Toronto . . .
Cities, countries, continents,
(stay in hotels, or in tents!)
talk to people, make new friends
for learning and fun that never ends.

Bulletin Board Tips

- Use light blue paper for the background and dark blue for the border.

- Decorate the border with flags, maps, and photos of the countries featured.

- Divide these flip-ups into four different sections based on continents and use a different color for each section.

26

Flip-up Ideas

You can prepare your flip-ups for this unit by either asking questions about different countries around the world or, as I have done, by selecting four continents and listing capitals underneath them.

[Instruction Card] *Do you know the capitals of these countries? Look in an atlas to help you find the answer. Then lift the flaps to find out!*

EUROPE	ASIA	NORTH AMERICA	AFRICA
■ France **Paris**	■ Turkey **Ankara**	■ Bahamas **Nassau**	■ Algeria **Algiers**
■ Greece **Athens**	■ China **Beijing**	■ Jamaica **Kingston**	■ Egypt **Cairo**
■ Italy **Rome**	■ Syria **Damascus**	■ Canada **Ottawa**	■ Kenya **Nairobi**
■ Portugal **Lisbon**	■ Vietnam **Hanoi**	■ Barbados **Bridgetown**	■ Liberia **Monrovia**
■ Norway **Oslo**	■ Israel **Jerusalem**	■ United States **Washington, D.C.**	■ Tunisia **Tunis**

Extensions

Younger Students: Explain that to travel to different countries, you need a passport—an official document that states what country you are from. Make passports out of folded pieces of construction paper, with children's pictures on the outside and the names of countries they would like to visit on the inside. Add these to the bulletin board.

Older Students: Have students imagine that they have three days to visit the country of their choice. Help them create an hour-by-hour itinerary that reflects how they would spend their time there.

Suggested Book Links

Let's Go Traveling by Robin Rector Krupp (Morrow Jr. Books, 1992). This fun fictional tale uses storytelling and photo collage to follow a young girl's trip through Europe, complete with schedules, tickets, postcards, and souvenirs.

The Steck-Vaughn Atlas of the World (Raintree Steck-Vaughn, 1995). This useful, current atlas will help students answer the flip-up questions and can be used as a springboard for discovering new information.

September • October • November • **December** • January • February • March • April • May • Ju

Holidays Around the World

December is a season of many holidays. This bulletin board celebrates the fact that different holidays are celebrated in a variety of ways around the world.

Getting Started

Read the poem aloud. Then ask students about the holidays celebrated by their families at this time of year. Make a list on the board, adding any that aren't mentioned. Your list might include: Christmas; Hanukkah; Kwanzaa, the African American harvest festival; Three Kings Day, a Latin American celebration; St. Lucia's Day, a Swedish festival of lights; and Divali, a Hindu holiday celebrated by lighting lanterns.

Bulletin Board Poem

DECEMBER CELEBRATIONS
Every year at just this time,
In cold and dark December,
Families around the world
All gather to remember.
With presents and parties
And feasting and fun,
Traditions and customs
for old and for young.
All over the world,
In all lands and nations,
People enjoy
December celebrations!

Bulletin Board Tips

■ Use a variety of holiday colors such as red, green, blue, and silver for the background and borders.

■ For this bulletin board, staple the flip-ups directly to the board and tape the poem to the wall next to the board.

28

Flip-up Ideas

These flip-ups introduce children to winter holidays around the world.

[Instruction Card] *Can you name the winter holidays described here? Lift the flaps for the answers!*

- People exchange presents in honor of the birth of Jesus.
Christmas

- Workers in England receive gifts on this day, December 26.
Boxing Day

- People in China celebrate this festival of peace and renewal each year.
Ta Chiu

- African Americans celebrate their heritage with this seven-day harvest festival.
Kwanzaa

- Hindu families set out lanterns to honor the goddess Lakshmi on this holiday.
Divali

- Children in Europe receive presents from a man with a long white beard on this day.
St. Nicholas Day

- People in many parts of the world celebrate the end of the old year and the beginning of a new one on this night.
New Year's Eve

- Girls wear wreaths of candles on the morning of this Swedish holiday.
St. Lucia's Day

- Jewish families celebrate this holiday by lighting candles for eight days.
Hanukkah

- In Spain and Latin America, children remember the Three Wise Men who visited Jesus.
Three Kings Day

Extensions

Younger Students: Invite someone from another country (perhaps the family member of a student) to speak to the class about holiday celebrations there.

Older Students: Have students research holidays in different countries and create a calendar, filling in as many holidays as students can find throughout the year.

Suggested Book Links

Celebrate the Season: Holiday Stories From Highlights by the Highlights Staff (Boyds Mills Press, 1994). This collection from the well-known children's magazine is a multicultural treasure trove of holiday stories.

My First Kwanzaa Book by Deborah M. Newton Chocolate (Scholastic, 1992). The story of this African American holiday is told very simply with beautiful pictures. The seven days of Kwanzaa and its traditions are explained.

September • October • November • December • **January** • February • March • April • May • Ju

Celebrate With Hats

Did you know that the third Friday in January is Hat Day? This topic links with history, careers, and even geography.

Getting Started

Read (or sing!) the poem aloud while wearing a hat you made or brought from home. Divide students into groups, and see how many different kinds of hats they can brainstorm. Your students may be surprised to realize how many different kinds of hats there are!

Bulletin Board Poem

HATS OFF TO HATS
(sing to the tune of "Home on the Range")

Oh, here are the hats,
People wear on their heads
In the winter and summer and fall—
They wear hats when they fish—
When they're cooking a dish—
Or when they want to look
Very tall!

Hats, hats on our heads!
There are hats people wear in bed!
Even under the ground,
Special hats can be found,
So let's hear it for the hats
on our heads!

Bulletin Board Tips

- Use blue paper for the background and white for the border.

- Decorate the board with cutout hat shapes, real hats (such as a sailor or straw hat bought at a costume store), or pictures of hats.

- Have students draw and cut out pictures of their favorite hats and write their names inside. Staple these hats to the bulletin board.

Flip-up Ideas

These flip-ups will introduce students to various kinds of hats.

[Instruction Card] *Use the clues to name each kind of hat. The answers are under the flaps.*

- This flat red hat is worn by men in Morocco and other Mediterranean countries.
Fez

- This round cap became popular in France.
Beret

- This wide-brimmed hat tops many heads in Mexico.
Sombrero

- This three-sided hat was popular during the American Revolution.
Tricorner

- This straw hat is named after a country in Central America.
Panama

- The nickname for this cowboy hat is a form of measurement.
Ten-gallon hat

- Many people like to wear this sports hat backward.
Baseball cap

- Workers wear these hard hats to keep their heads safe from harm.
Helmets

- This hat with strings was worn by prairie girls.
Bonnet

- This black hat is worn with a tuxedo.
Top hat

Extensions

Younger Students: Celebrate Hat Day with a special Hat Parade. Choose a theme like Hats From History or Hats Around the World, and help students make hats out of paper.

Older Students: Use hats as an opportunity to practice map skills with students. Use a world map, and make a map key showing hats that are popular in different areas of the world.

Suggested Book Links

Abe Lincoln's Hat by Martha Brenner (Random House, 1994). An interesting read for children that tells the story of the stovepipe that President Lincoln wore. Children will enjoy learning that he hid papers and other objects under his hat!

Hats Hats Hats by Ann Morris (Lothrop, Lee & Shepard, 1989). Readers learn about hats worn by people around the world. There is a very good index and beautiful photos that show people wearing different hats.

We Have Dreams, Too!

Martin Luther King Day is celebrated the third Monday in January. This bulletin board celebrates his dreams of peace and tolerance.

Getting Started

Depending on how familiar your students are with Dr. King, you may wish to read aloud a short biography about him along with the poem. Explain to students that Dr. King dreamed of a world in which all people were treated equally, and he worked hard to achieve that dream.

Bulletin Board Poem

MARTIN LUTHER KING, JR.
When Martin Luther King
was just a tiny little boy,
His parents taught him
to be brave and true.
His parents taught him very well,
and when young Martin grew,
Martin learned to be a dreamer, too.
Martin was a dreamer,
Martin dreamed of peace.
Martin dreamed a dream
for you and me.
Martin had a dream
that all the children of the world
would live in freedom and equality.

Bulletin Board Tips

- Use blue paper for the background and red for the border.

- Decorate the board with photographs and/or pictures of Dr. King.

- What dreams for the world do your students have? Cut pieces of construction paper into simple human shapes. Have each student write his or her dream on a figure and staple the figures to the bulletin board.

I HAVE A DREAM!

Flip-up Ideas

These questions will help children learn more about Martin Luther King, Jr.

[Instruction Card] *Do you know the answers to these questions about Martin Luther King, Jr.? A library is a good place to look for the answers!*

- When was Martin Luther King, Jr., born? **January 15, 1929**

- What prize did he win in 1964 for his efforts in the peace movement? **The Nobel peace prize**

- What was Martin Luther King, Jr.'s, dream? **That all people live in peace and harmony, and be treated equally**

- Where did Dr. King and 200,000 of his followers hold their most famous march for peace? **Washington, D.C.**

- At what age did he graduate from high school? **Age 15**

- Whom did he marry? **Coretta Scott King**

- Where did he grow up? **Atlanta, Georgia**

- What did both his father and grandfather do? **They were both preachers.**

- What famous peacemaker did Dr. King model himself on? **Mahatma Gandhi**

- What woman started the bus boycott in Montgomery, Alabama, in 1955? **Rosa Parks**

Extensions

Younger Students: Use Dr. King's message of peace as an opportunity to practice conflict resolution with your students. Act out situations with your students (such as cutting in line or fighting over a toy), and discuss peaceful ways to solve the kinds of conflicts they face each day.

Older Students: Invite students to write biographies of Dr. King or another person they consider to be a hero.

Suggested Book Links

Happy Birthday, Martin Luther King by Jean Marzollo (Scholastic, 1994). This easy-to-read book is filled with facts, and is illustrated by J. Brian Pinkney. (A Spanish-language version is also available.)

Martin Luther King, Jr. by Maria Fleming (Scholastic, 1995). A sensitively written teaching resource that helps children understand the role Dr. King played in shaping our nation's history. Includes reproducible maps, songs, plays, primary source materials, and literature links, as well as role-playing and conflict-resolution activities.

President's Month

President's Month was originally designed in honor of George Washington and Abraham Lincoln, who were both born in February. It has become a month in which we honor all the former presidents who served our country.

Getting Started

Read the poem, and ask students to name the current president of the United States. Find out how many of the remaining presidents students can name from memory.

Bulletin Board Poem

PRESIDENT'S MONTH

If I were pres-i-dent,
I'll tell you what I'd do;
I'd help to make our country run,
Our land of the red, white, and blue.

If I were pres-i-dent,
(and this I know for sure)
I'd treat all people fairly,
young or old, and rich or poor.

If I had that job, I'd try hard to be the very best president in history!

Bulletin Board Tips

- You can purchase red, white, and blue star bordettes at a teacher supply store.

- Staple a picture of the current president to the board, or use pictures of George Washington and Abraham Lincoln.

Flip-up Ideas

Use these flip-up questions to get you started. Students can easily create additional flip-ups by researching other facts about the presidents.

[Instruction Card] *Can you name these presidents? Their names are under the flaps.*

- He was the first president of the United States.
George Washington

- His daughter, Susanna, was the first child to live in the White House. **John Adams**

- His face is on a penny.
Abraham Lincoln

- His pet parrot could whistle "Yankee Doodle."
William McKinley

- The Teddy Bear was named after this president.
Theodore Roosevelt

- He was nicknamed "The Red Fox" because of his bright red hair.
Thomas Jefferson

- He was the only president to be sworn into office on an airplane.
Lyndon B. Johnson

- At 5 feet 4 inches tall, he was the shortest president.
James Madison

- He worked as a newspaper editor before he became president.
Warren G. Harding

- This president had 15 children.
John Tyler

Extension

All Students: If students could talk to the president, what would they ask? Have students turn their questions into letters and mail them to the president. They will probably receive a reply along with some information about the presidency. Write to:

> The President
> The White House
> Washington, DC 20500

Suggested Book Links

Facts and Fun About the Presidents by George Sullivan (Scholastic, 1987). This book is brimming with presidential trivia perfect for flip-ups.

Step-Up Biographies series (Random House). This series offers easy-to-read biographies of George Washington, Abraham Lincoln, Thomas Jefferson, and John F. Kennedy.

Let's Be Heart Smart

While students are thinking of valentine hearts, you can create this bulletin board to help teach the science of the human body.

Getting Started

What do students already know about the heart? Read the poem aloud. Then make a list of heart facts on the board or on a heart-shaped piece of oaktag. Students can make small, heart-shaped flip-ups to add to the bulletin board. Have each student write his or her name on the outside and a heart fact on the inside.

Bulletin Board Poem

HEART SMART

It's very smart
to take care of your heart—
It's the muscle with hustle,
and that's just the start!

So make sure you eat right
and get exercise;
'cause that's the best way
to become heart-wise!

Bulletin Board Tips

- Use white construction paper for the background and red for the border.

- Make the flip-ups in heart shapes. Use pink construction paper so that the writing is visible.

- A chart or diagram labeling the heart and its parts adds interest and information to the board.

Flip-up Ideas

A fill-in-the-blank format makes these questions accessible to most students, especially if you post a list of possible answers next to the flip-ups.

[Instruction Card] *Can you fill in the blanks in these heart-smart sentences? Lift up the flaps to learn the answers!*

- The heart is a strong _____ inside the chest.
  muscle

- The heart pumps _____ to other parts of the body.
  blood

- The heart is located on the _____ side of your body.
  left

- Your heart is about the size of your _____.
  fist

- A child's heart beats about _____ times per minute.
  65 to 130

- Blood enters the heart through special tubes called _____.
  veins

- Blood leaves the heart through special tubes called _____.
  arteries

- Your heart beats fastest when you _____.
  exercise

- Your heart beats slowest when you _____.
  sleep

- _____ makes your heart stronger.
  Exercise

Extensions

Younger Students: Make a stethoscope by attaching about 12 inches of plastic tubing (available in home-repair or plumbing-supply stores) to the cut-off top of a plastic detergent bottle. Students can hold the tube to their ears and press the bottle top to their chests to listen and count their heartbeats.

Older Students: Trace the outline of a student's entire body on a large sheet of art paper. Have students work together to draw and label as many parts of the body as they can. Post the finished work next to the bulletin board.

Suggested Book Links

The Body Book: Easy-to-Make, Hands-on Models That Teach by Donald M. Silver and Patricia J. Wynne (Scholastic, 1993). This book contains reproducible cut-and-paste patterns for assembling and understanding the parts of the human body.

The Magic School Bus Inside the Human Body by Joanna Cole (Scholastic, 1989). Ms. Frizzle and her class explore the heart when they go on a field trip through the human body.

Women in History

Celebrate Women's History Month with a bulletin board that highlights the achievements of great women.

📓 Getting Started

Use the poem to start a discussion about famous women children may be familiar with. Younger children can draw pictures of famous women they are aware of and write a short sentence about them. Older students can research and write a short biographical paragraph about a woman of their choice. Staple the pictures and biographies to the bulletin board.

📓 Bulletin Board Poem

WOMEN'S HISTORY

Why do they call it "his-story?"
It's really quite a mystery!
It should be hers-and-history
if you ask me!
'Cause women like Harriet Tubman
helped people to be free!
And women got to vote with help
from Susan B. Anthony!
History was made by hims and hers,
In this land of equal opportunity!

📓 Bulletin Board Tip

■ Use yellow construction paper for the background and red for the border.

Flip-up Ideas

Your students will enjoy these "Who Am I?" riddles.

[Instruction Card] *Can you guess who these famous women are? Lift the flaps to find out!*

- I was a volunteer nurse called the "Angel of the Battlefield." I organized the American Red Cross. Who am I? **Clara Barton**

- I led many slaves to freedom on the Underground Railroad. Who am I? **Harriet Tubman**

- I became the first American woman to travel in space in 1983. Who am I? **Sally Ride**

- I was a Powhatan princess who helped early European settlers who came to this land. Who am I? **Pocahontas**

- I was the first woman to fly solo over the Pacific Ocean. Who am I? **Amelia Earhart**

- I was a first lady who worked hard to improve human rights and became a U.S. delegate to the United Nations. Who am I? **Eleanor Roosevelt**

- Even though I had polio as a child, I grew up to win four Olympic track medals. Who am I? **Wilma Rudolph**

- I became blind and deaf when I was a baby. I grew up and spoke out for others with physical challenges. Who am I? **Helen Keller**

- I fought for women to have the right to vote. You can now see my face on a dollar coin. Who am I? **Susan B. Anthony**

Extensions

Younger Students: Encourage students to create picture books that illustrate the major events in the life of a famous woman of their choice. Collect the class books on a Women's History bookshelf.

Older Students: Students can create timelines based on the women featured on the flip-ups. Have students research the dates. Then display finished timelines in the bulletin board area.

Suggested Book Links

A Picture Book of Harriet Tubman by David A. Adler (Holiday House, 1992). This lavishly illustrated book is a wonderful introduction to the biography format for younger students, featuring one of the most famous women in our country's history.

They Led the Way: Fourteen American Women by Johanna Johnson (Scholastic, 1992). Older students will enjoy reading about some of the greatest women in U.S. history, including Clara Barton and Abigail Adams.

Buzzing With Insects!

Children are always fascinated to learn about these crawly creatures. They'll be buzzing around this high-interest bulletin board!

Getting Started

Use the poem to start a discussion about insects. What are students' first thoughts when they think of insects? Are they afraid of them? Do they think they're pests? Introduce the idea that many insects are helpful to humans and to the planet, like bees and silkworms. Students will have a chance to learn more about harmful and helpful animals when they explore the bulletin board.

Bulletin Board Poem

INSECTS

When the weather gets warm
what do I see?
A buzzing swarm
of pesty bees!
Or maybe ants,
or flies,
or fleas,
oh, go away bugs!
Don't bug me, please!
You can pollinate flowers,
make honey for hours,
but keep away from me—please!

Bulletin Board Tips

- Use yellow construction paper for the background and a green insect bordette (available at a teacher supply store).

- Make the flip-ups in butterfly shapes using the template on page 42. Use yellow paper, and attach pipe cleaners for the antennae.

- Draw or tape a picture of each insect next to its name on the flip-up.

Flip-up Ideas

These flip-ups review different kinds of helpful and harmful insects.

[Instruction Card] *Are these insects harmful or helpful to humans and the planet? Lift the flap to find out!*

- Silkworms
Helpful. They make silk that humans use to make clothing.

- Bees
Helpful. They make honey. They only sting to protect themselves from enemies.

- Ladybugs
Helpful. They eat large numbers of harmful insects.

- Butterflies
Helpful. They carry pollen from flower to flower. That helps new plants grow.

- Houseflies
Harmful. Some kinds carry diseases that can make humans sick.

- Termites
Harmful. They chew on wood. That can hurt houses, bridges, and boats.

- Moths
Harmful. They destroy cereal, grains, and clothes.

- Weevils
Harmful. Many kinds of weevils eat crops and trees.

Extensions

Younger Students: If possible, take students on an insect hunt in the neighborhood. Have them keep a record of how many different kinds of insects and other bugs you find. Use a field guide to insects to help identify unfamiliar creatures.

Older Students: Students can use pictures or photos of insects to practice labeling. Have students locate and label the three major body parts of each insect: the head, thorax, and abdomen. Then have them label any other parts they find: wings, eyes, legs, antennae. Add the diagrams to the bulletin board.

Suggested Book Links

Insects and Spiders by Paul Hillyard (Dorling Kindersley, 1993). This publisher's exciting style of presenting information works well with the subject matter, as readers are treated to pages of photos, facts, and diagrams of all kinds of bugs.

The Bug Book by Robin Bernard (Scholastic, 1995). Everything you need to launch a theme unit on the topic of bugs: background information, hands-on activities and experiments, games, mini-books, and more.

BUTTERFLY TEMPLATE

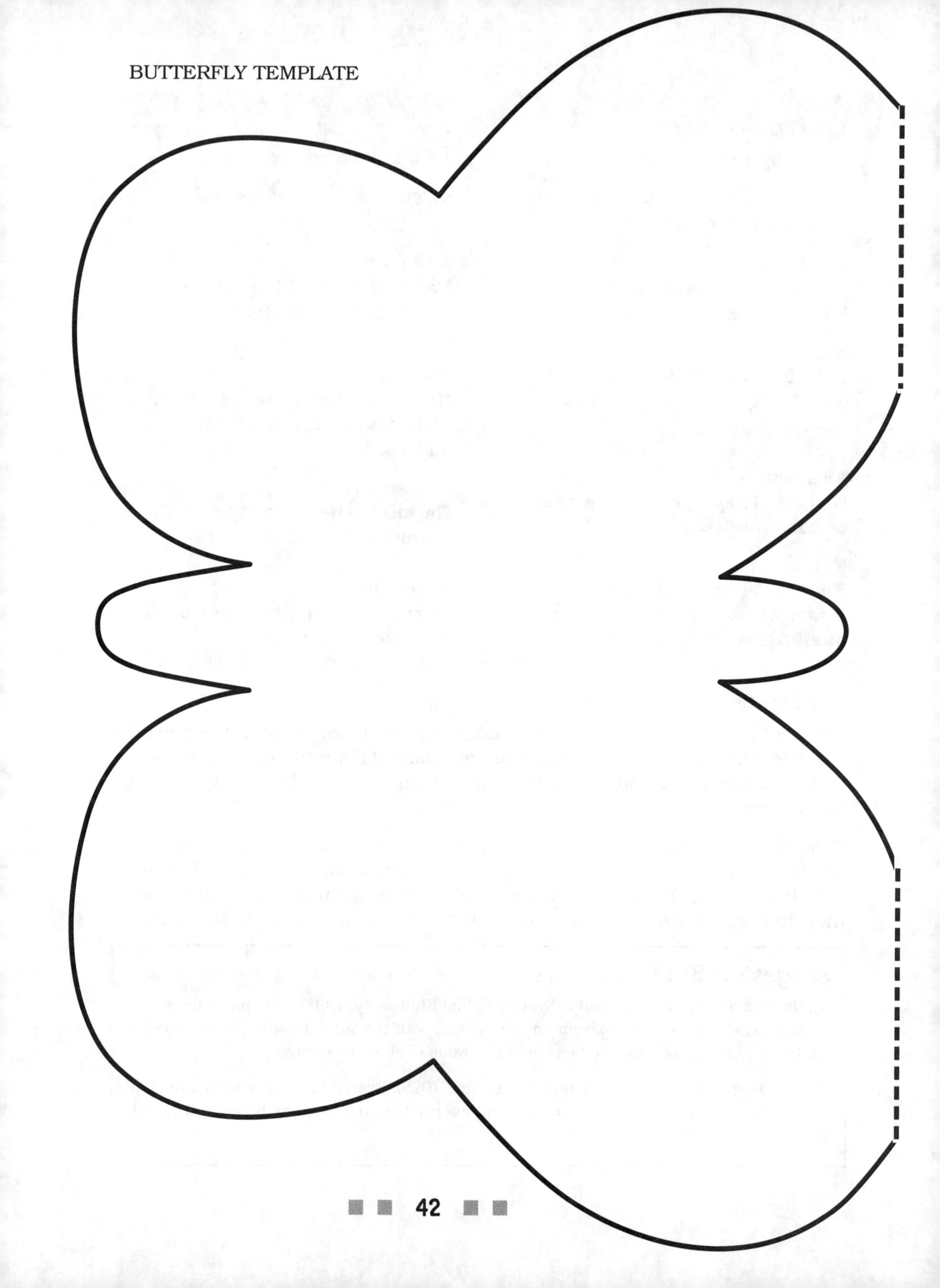

42

… September • October • November • December • January • February • March • **April** • May • June

Get Well Soon, Planet Earth!

Earth Day gives us the opportunity to celebrate the beauty of our planet. This bulletin board introduces children to the issues they need to know about protecting the earth and keeping it healthy.

Getting Started

Ask students to name some of the ways in which the earth is "not well" that are mentioned in the poem. Make a list on the board. Then challenge students to add other ideas.

Reassure children that people everywhere are working to help the earth. Everyone can do something. Start by making "Get Well" cards for the earth. Students can include ideas for helping the earth in their cards. Attach the finished cards to the bulletin board.

Bulletin Board Poem

GET WELL SOON, PLANET EARTH

Planet Earth is ailing,
Planet Earth's not well.
She's sick of smog,
She's sick of trash
and other things as well.
But Planet Earth's our mother,
so we'll work with all our might—
to do the things we need to
'til she's back to feeling right.

Bulletin Board Tips

- Use blue construction paper for the background and yellow for the border.

- Make the flip-ups in the shape of the earth. If you have Earth Day stickers, add them to the front of the flip-ups.

43

Flip-up Ideas

Test your students' environmental IQ with these flip-ups.

[Instruction Card] *There are many ways to help the earth get well. Which of these choices is better for the planet? Lift the flaps to find out.*

- Take the bus or drive a car? **Take the bus! You'll save energy.**

- Use a glass or paper cup? **Use a glass! Paper cups create more garbage.**

- Take a three-minute shower or a ten-minute shower? **Take a three-minute shower! It's important to conserve water.**

- Buy apples wrapped in plastic or loose in a crate? **Buy them loose! Always look for products with as little packaging as possible.**

- Ride the elevator or take the stairs? **Take the stairs! You'll save energy.**

- Cool off with a fan or an air conditioner? **Cool off with a fan! It produces fewer pollutants.**

- Throw away that soda can or recycle it? **Recycle it! You'll help keep garbage out of landfills.**

- Pack groceries in a canvas bag or paper bag? **Pack them in a canvas bag! You can use it again and again.**

Extension

All Students: Your students may already be familiar with the book *50 Simple Things Kids Can Do to Save the Planet* (Earthworks Group, 1991). Make a class version of this book, using your students' ideas and suggestions.

Suggested Book Links

Long Live Earth by Meighan Morrison (Scholastic, 1994). This book uses a poetic format to present some of the destructive things people have done to the planet and suggests ways that we can make things better. An excellent resource to introduce the topic.

The Lorax by Dr. Seuss (Random House, 1971). Younger readers will especially love this classic tale of the harmful effects of pollution. Readers of all ages will be captivated by the illustrations and wordplay.

September • October • November • December • January • February • March • **April** • May • June

Animals in Danger

These flip-ups will teach children fascinating facts about endangered animals.

Getting Started

Make two columns on the chalkboard: Things That Harm Animals and Things That Help Animals. Then read the poem and ask: Why do you think many of the world's animals are in danger of becoming extinct? (Review the vocabulary words *endangered* and *extinct* with younger students at this point.) Ask students to offer reasons why some animals are in danger and some ways in which animals are being helped. List their reasons in the columns on the board.

Bulletin Board Poem

ANIMALS IN DANGER
They cannot speak,
they cannot talk,
(except to roar, or grunt, or squawk).
Endangered animals can't remind us
to put our careless ways behind us.
So we'll remind ourselves to care
for animal habitats everywhere.

Bulletin Board Tips

- Use green construction paper for the background. Animal bordettes are available at teacher supply stores.

- Attach pictures of endangered animals to the board.

- Add a picture or sticker of each animal to the outside flap of the flip-ups.

45

Flip-up Ideas

These facts will spark children's interest in learning more about endangered animals.

[Instruction Card] *Can you name these endangered animals? Lift up the flaps for the answers.*

- This animal travels in packs of 5 to 20 animals. **Wolf**

- This animal sleeps floating on water, wrapped in seaweed. **Sea otter**

- This desert animal can carry more than 450 pounds on its back. **Bactrian camel**

- This nearly extinct bird is the largest bird of prey in North America. **California condor**

- This animal weighs between 175 and 225 pounds at birth. **African elephant**

- The bamboo forests that this monkeylike animal calls home are being destroyed. **Aye-aye**

- This endangered creature is the largest and heaviest animal on the planet. **Blue whale**

- This sea creature is hunted for its skin and shell. **Ridley sea turtle**

- This spotted African cat is the fastest animal alive. **Cheetah**

- This striped cat lives in the rain forests and jungles of Asia. **Tiger**

Extensions

Younger Students: Use a world map to identify where the endangered animals on the flip-ups live. Have students work as a class to create an endangered animals map and a map key.

Older Students: Connect this topic to your social studies curriculum by having students research the endangered animals that live in your state.

Suggested Book Links

I Am Leaper by Annabel Johnson (Scholastic, 1990). This easy chapter book tells the story of a kangaroo rat who enlists the help of a young boy to protect her desert home.

Protecting Endangered Species at the San Diego Zoo by Georgeanne Irvine (Simon and Schuster, 1990). Readers learn about some of the programs that have been set up to help endangered animals. It's a positive lesson in problem solving.

Keep Fit and Healthy

May is National Physical Fitness Month. This bulletin board encourages children to eat right and stay physically fit.

Getting Started

The poem will introduce students to the two basics of keeping fit: exercise and good nutrition. Have students keep a diary of the food they eat and the exercise they get in one day. Use your own diary or a sample you make up, and analyze it as a class. Then have students analyze their own diaries. What changes could they make to create a healthier lifestyle?

Bulletin Board Poem

KEEP FIT AND HEALTHY

Put on your sneakers
Come out and run!
'Cause keeping fit
is lots of fun!

Put fruits and vegetables
in your lunch pack!
'Cause healthy food
makes a great snack!

Exercising
and eating right
keeps you healthy
day and night!

Bulletin Board Tips

- Use yellow construction paper for the background and red for the border.

- Decorate the bulletin board with paper cut into the shapes of a plate, utensils, place mat, and napkin.

- Make the flip-ups in the shape of a sneaker using the template on page 49. Tie real shoelaces through the eyelets.

Flip-up Ideas

This fact or fiction exercise is a good way to explore students' beliefs about nutrition and fitness. (For younger students, you may wish to use true or false.)

[Instruction Card] *Are these statements Fitness Facts or Fitness Fiction? Make a guess. Then lift the flaps to find out!*

- Everyone should do the same exercises. **Fiction**

- An apple a day will keep the doctor away. **Fiction**

- There is a right way to do most exercises. **Fact**

- All thin people are healthy. **Fiction**

- If you exercise once a week, you will be healthy. **Fiction**

- It's good to eat lots of vegetables. **Fact**

- It's good to eat lots of sugar. **Fiction**

- Drink all the milk you want to get healthy bones. **Fiction**

- Potato chips are a healthy snack. **Fiction**

- Even children need to exercise. **Fact**

Extensions

Younger Students: Exercise can be fun! Divide students into groups and have them invent a new game that involves some kind of physical activity—running, jumping, etc. They can write rules for the game and teach other groups how it's played.

Older Students: If you have access to a video camera, create a class fitness video with segments on exercise and nutrition. Students can also work together to create a fitness magazine, complete with tips, advice, and instructions for exercising and eating right.

Suggested Book Links

Be the Best—Fun & Fitness by Sheila Rich (Troll Associates, 1990). This step-by-step guide is filled with activities that will help young people become physically fit.

The Food Cycle by David Smith (Thomson Learning, 1993). This book covers the proper foods we should eat to stay healthy, and tells us where foods come from and how they are processed around the world.

SNEAKER TEMPLATE

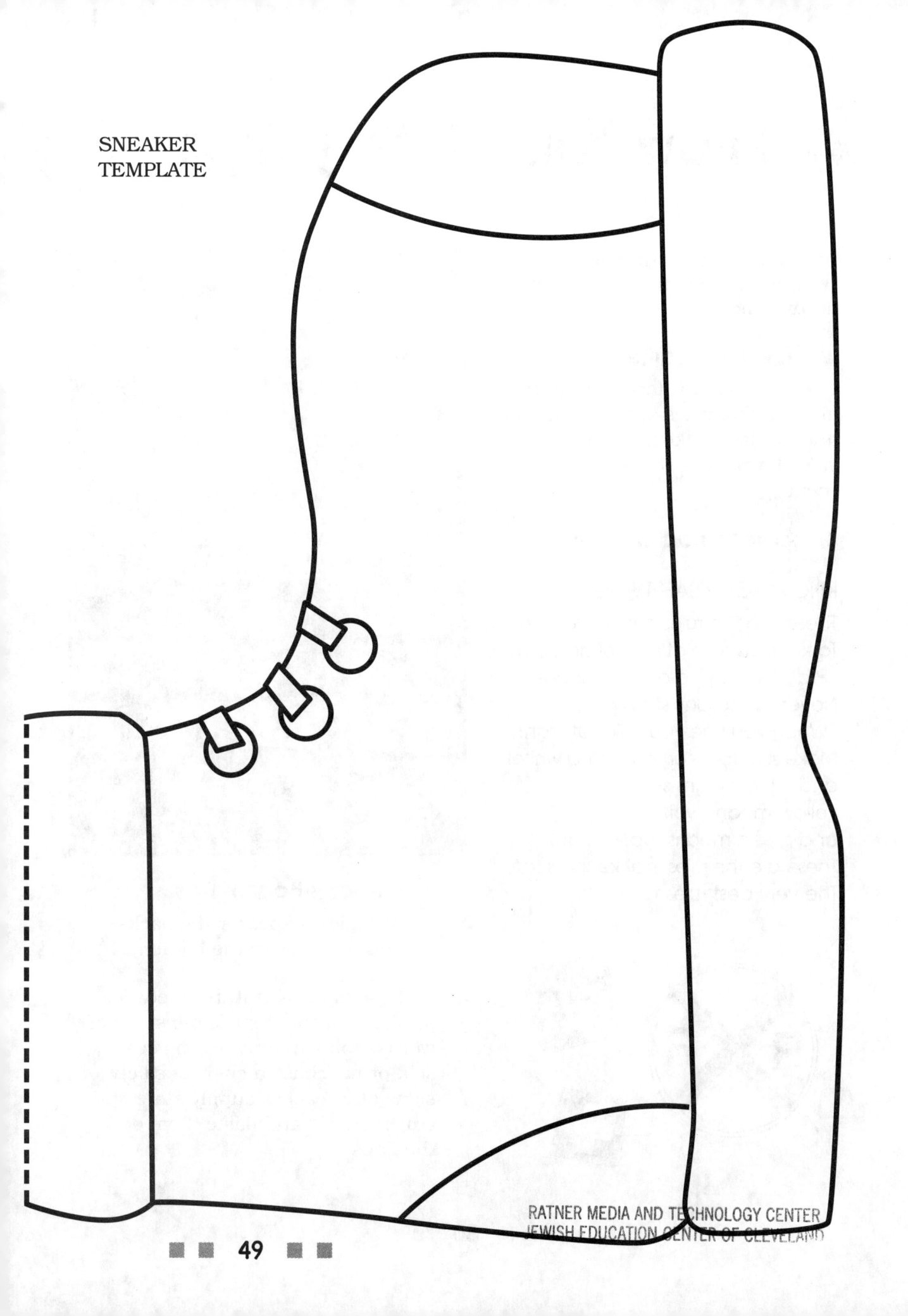

49

September • October • November • December • January • February • March • April • **May** • Jun

Know Your Safety Signs

This bulletin board makes children aware of the safety signs around them.

📄 Getting Started

Use the poem to start a discussion about safety rules at home, school, and at play. Make a list of safety rules for the classroom and post them.

📄 Bulletin Board Poem

KNOW YOUR SAFETY SIGNS

These are the rules that we obey,
To keep us safe at school and play:
"Practice staying out of danger.
Never talk to any stranger!"
"When you ride your bike at night,
Make sure to wear something white!"
and "Red means stop,
yellow means wait,
and green means, go, go, go!"
These are the rules that keep us safe,
The very best rules to know.

📄 Bulletin Board Tips

- Use yellow paper for the background and red for the border.

- These flip-ups feature safety symbols on the front flap instead of words. You can draw them yourself, or purchase a chart of safety signs at a teacher supply store and cut them out and paste them on the flaps.

50

Flip-up Ideas

Will children recognize the safety symbols on these flip-ups? When they're done, they should be safety experts!

[Instruction Card] *What do each of these safety symbols mean? Lift the flaps for the answers.*

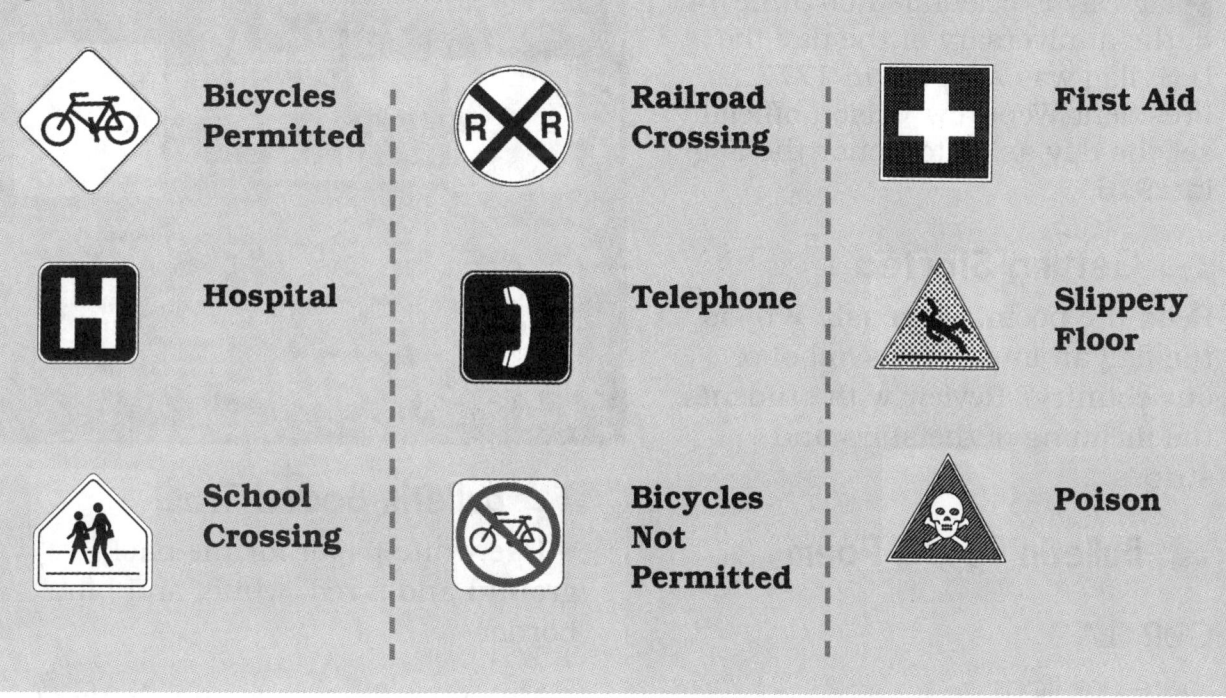

Bicycles Permitted	Railroad Crossing	First Aid
Hospital	Telephone	Slippery Floor
School Crossing	Bicycles Not Permitted	Poison

Extension

All Students: Write to the National Safe Kids Campaign for tips and materials you can share with your students. Then invite students to work in groups to create their own safety tip pamphlets about various topics. Write to:

> **National Safe Kids Campaign, Dept. NSKW Ideas**
> **11 Michigan Ave. NW**
> **Washington, DC 20010-2970**

Suggested Book Links

Scooter by Vera B. Williams (Greenwillow, 1993). This illustrated chapter book is the fictional story of a young girl who lives in a city apartment building. Events in the book could lead to discussions about safety practices during play.

The Street Smart Book by William Marsano (Wanderer Books, 1985). This book discusses dangerous situations children might encounter and offers appropriate strategies for dealing with them. This is an excellent source for safety in the streets.

Celebrating Our Flag

Flag Day is celebrated on June 14, the anniversary of the day the U.S. flag was adopted in 1777. President Woodrow Wilson officially set the day aside to honor the flag in 1916.

Getting Started

Read the poem. Then ask: Why is the flag an important symbol of our country? Review with students the meaning of the stars and stripes.

Bulletin Board Poem

OUR FLAG

There are flags
the whole world over,
and each flag is really great!
But there is really only one
I want to celebrate—
With its 50 stars on a field of blue
and its 13 stripes
for the brave and true,
it's the flag that tells
our nation's story—
the banner that we call Old Glory!

Bulletin Board Tips

- Use white paper for the background and a red, white, and blue border.

- Make the flip-ups in the shape of a flag. Add flag stickers to the outside flap to add interest.

- Decorate the board with red, white, and blue bows or streamers.

Flip-up Ideas

These questions and answers about the flag can be used on your flip-ups.

[Instruction Card] *Do you know these flag facts? Lift the flaps to learn the answers.*

- What are the colors of our flag? **Red, white, and blue**

- Which president designated Flag Day to be celebrated on June 14? **President Woodrow Wilson, in 1916**

- How many stripes does our flag have? **13 (7 red and 6 white)**

- Who wrote the Pledge of Allegiance? **Francis Bellamy**

- When did children first begin to recite the Pledge of Allegiance in school? **1892**

- What other names does the flag have? **Old Glory, Stars and Stripes, Star Spangled Banner**

- Who wrote "The Star Spangled Banner"? **Francis Scott Key**

- How many stars does our flag have? **50**

- When was our flag adopted as the official flag of the United States? **1777**

- When were the last two stars added to the flag? **In 1959, when Hawaii and Alaska became states**

Extension

All Students: Create additional flip-ups based on other symbols of the United States: the bald eagle, the Liberty Bell, the Statue of Liberty, etc.

Suggested Book Links

I Pledge Allegiance by June Swanson (On My Own Books, Carolrhoda, 1990). A look at the history behind the Pledge of Allegiance in an easy-to-grasp format for younger students.

If You Were There When They Signed the Constitution by Elizabeth Levy (Scholastic, 1992). What was life like when our country was formed and the flag was made? This book will answer children's questions.

September • October • November • December • January • February • March • April • May • **Jun**

I Want to Leave You Laughing

After a school year of learning and hard work, a good way for students to get ready for summer vacation is with jokes, riddles, and humorous books to read. These flip-ups will get them started!

Getting Started

Read the poem aloud. Then ask students to share riddles that they know with the class. Students can become very involved in creating this bulletin board. You may wish to have them create the flip-up riddles themselves.

Bulletin Board Poem

I WANT TO LEAVE YOU LAUGHING

I want to leave you laughing,
now that school is almost done.
See if you can guess the answers
to these riddles, just for fun:

What has a hand
but no arm?
Sometimes it gives
an alarm.
A clock

What has an eye,
but never blinks?
A needle

What has a tongue,
but never drinks?
A shoe

Bulletin Board Tips

- Use pink paper for the background. Clown bordettes are available at teacher supply stores.

- Add smiling faces or clown stickers to the outer flap of the flip-ups.

- Decorate the bulletin board with clown faces.

Hee-Hee-Hee!

HA-HA-HA!

Tee-Hee-Hee!

54

Flip-up Ideas

These funny flip-ups are guaranteed to get laughs from anyone who reads them. This bulletin board is a great way to end the school year.

[Instruction Card] *Can you guess the answers to these riddles? Flip the flaps if you're stumped!*

- What are two words that have thousands of letters in them? **Post office**

- What is the best way to talk to a monster? **Long distance**

- Who won the race between the carrot and the lettuce? **The lettuce, because it was a-head.**

- Why was the cornstalk angry with the farmer? **Because the farmer kept pulling its ears.**

- How can you eat and learn at the same time? **Eat alphabet soup and learn the letters.**

- What do you say to a 100-year-old ghost? **Happy birthday to you-whoooooooooooo!**

- What makes more squeaking noises than a mouse? **Two mice**

- What is black and white and red all over? **A blushing zebra**

- What is an elephant after it is four months old? **Five months old**

- What key won't fit into a door? **A tur<u>key</u>**

- What is the best month of the year to hold a parade? **March**

Extensions

Younger Students: Invite students to illustrate some of their favorite riddles from the bulletin board.

Older Students: Hold a riddle game show in which students try to stump one another with riddles. Set up a display of riddle and joke books for students to use.

Suggested Book Links

Give a Dog a Bone compiled by Joanna Cole and Stephanie Calmenson (Scholastic, 1996). A collection of stories, poems, jokes, and riddles about dogs, featuring contributors such as author Frank Asch and illustrator John Speirs.

The Wackiest Nature Riddles on Earth by Mike Artelly (Sterling, 1993). A fun read, especially for those interested in science.